DAD JOKES

....

....

DON'T TELL MOM.

Why don't skeletons fight each other?
They don't have the guts.

Did you hear about the cheese factory explosion?
There was nothing left but de-brie.

I'm reading a book on anti-gravity.
It's impossible to put down.

What do you call fake spaghetti?
An impasta.

I told my wife she should embrace
her mistakes.
She gave me a hug.

Why don't scientists trust atoms?
Because they make up everything.

What do you call a fish wearing a bowtie?
SoFISHticated.

I'm on a seafood diet.
I see food and I eat it.

Why did the scarecrow win an award?
Because he was outstanding in his field.

What do you get when you cross
a snowman and a vampire?
Frostbite.

Why couldn't the bicycle stand up
by itself?
It was two-tired.

I used to play piano by ear,
but now I use my hands.

Why don't skeletons go to scary movies?
They don't have the guts.

What do you call a bear with no teeth?
A gummy bear.

I told my wife she was drawing
her eyebrows too high.
She looked surprised.

Why did the tomato turn red?
Because it saw the salad dressing.

How does a penguin build its house?
Igloos it together.

Why was the math book sad?
Because it had too many problems.

I told my computer I needed a break.
Now it won't stop sending me
vacation ads.

What do you call an alligatorwearing
a vest?
An investigator.

Why did the golfer bring two pairs
of pants?
In case he got a hole in one.

Why was the belt arrested?
It held up a pair of pants.

What did one ocean say to the other ocean?
Nothing, they just waved.

What did the janitor say when he jumped out of the closet?
"Supplies!"

What did the fish say when it hit the wall?
Dam!

I'm reading a book on the history of glue.
I just can't seem to put it down.

I used to be a baker,
but I couldn't make enough dough.

I'm trying to organize a hide and seek competition,
but it's difficult to find good players.

Did you hear about the kidnapping
at the playground?
They woke up.

I'm addicted to collecting vintage
dictionaries. I just can't stop,
I find it very hard to put them down.

What do you call a fake noodle?
An impasta!

I'm on a whiskey diet.
I've lost three days already.

Why did the bicycle fall over?
It was two-tired.

I'm writing a book about reverse psychology.
Please don't buy it.

What do you call a cow with no legs?
Ground beef.

I'm terrified of elevators,
so I'm taking steps to avoid them.

What do you call a can opener
that doesn't work?
A can't opener.

I used to have a job at a calendar factory
but I got the sack because I took a couple
of days off.

What do you call a pile of cats?
A meowtain.

Why don't eggs tell jokes?
Because they might crack up.

What did the grape say when it got stepped on?
Nothing, it just let out a little wine.

What did the ocean say to the shore?
Nothing, it just waved.

What did one plate say to the other plate?
Dinner's on me.

What's orange and sounds like a parrot?
A carrot.

What do you call fake cheese?
Nacho cheese.

What do you call a belt made out of watches?
A waist of time.

What's brown and sticky?
A stick.

Why did the chicken cross the playground?
To get to the other slide.

Why did the old man fall down the well?
He couldn't see that well.

I tried to make up a joke about ghost
but I couldn't.
It had plenty of spirit but no body.

Today at the bank, an old lady asked me
to check her balance... So I pushed her
over.

I got an A on my origami assignment when I turned my paper into my teacher.

How many storm troopers does it take to change a lightbulb?None, because they are all on the dark side.

Hi, I'm Cliff. Drop over sometime.

Dad, when he puts the car in reverse: "Ah, this takes me back."

What do you call the security guards for Samsung?
Guardians of the galaxy.

I was making a joke about retirement.
It did not work.

The other day I bought a thesaurus, but when I got home and opened it, all the pages were blank. I have no word to describe how angry I am.

The owner of the tuxedo store kept hovering over me when i was browsing, so I asked him to leave me alone. He said, "Fine, suit yourself."

Why did the egg have a day off?
Because it was Fryday.

Have you ever heard about the kidnapping at school? It's okay, he woke up.

Why did the coffee taste like dirt? Because it was ground just a few minutes ago.

Why did the Rolling Stones stop making music? Because they got to bottom of the hill.

What is the best present?
Broken drums! You can't beat them.

I made song about tortilla once,
now it's more like a wrap.

Did you know courdury pillows
are in style?
They're making headlines.

What does a nosey pepper do?
It gets jalapeño business.

Did you hear about the fragile myth?
It was busted.

What word can you make shorter
by adding two letters?
Short.

What do call a criminal landing
an airplane?
Condescending.

I stayed up all night wondering where
the sun went, and then it dawned on me.

Why do people who live in Greece hate
waking up at dawn?
Because Dawn is tough on Greece.

How do you make holy water?
You boil the hell out of it.

Justice is a dish best served cold.
Otherwise, it's just water.

Why should you never throw grandpa's
false teeth at a vehicle?
You might denture car.

Why are Christmas trees bad at knitting?
They always drop their needles.

What did the lunch box say to the
refrigerator? Don't hate me because
I'm a little cooler.

What do you do to have a space party?
You planet.

Why couldn't the tree get on his computer?
Because he could not log on.

What's a skeleton's favorite type of road?
A dead end.

What did the grape say when it got stepped on?
Nothing, just a little wine.

What did the alien say to the landscaper?
Take me to your weeder.

Me: "I want to write when I grow up."
Dad: "Why don't you left instead?"

How many apples grow on an apple tree?
All of them.

What did Elvis say to his landscaper?
Thank you for the mulch!

Why didn't the lifeguard save the hippie?
He was too far out!

What did the mother broom say
to the baby broom?
Time to go to sweep.

The other day I was attacked by a bunch of circus clowns in a parking lot. I won though, cause I went right for the juggler.

I'd like to shout out sidewalks for keeping me off the streets.

What did the computer go to the doctor? Because he had a virus.

How many ears does Captain Kirk have?
Three. The left ear, the right ear,
and the final front-ear.

Did you hear about the famous pickle?
He's a really big dill.

What do you need to make a highway in
an art studio?
A mile marker.

How does Vin Diesel keep in touch
with the Fast and Furious crew?
On a Zoom call.

What has four wheels and flies?
A garbage truck.

How much does a chimney cost.
Nothing, it's on the house.

Why do only some couples go to the gym?
Because some relationships don't work out.

You don't need a parachute
to go skydiving.
You need one to go skydiving twice.

Why is sausage bad for you?
It brings out the Wurst in people.

What do you call a broken clock?
A waste of time.

Why did the teddy bear turn down a slice of cake.
He was stuffed.

What's an astronaut's favorite board game?
Moon-opoly

How do you make Budweiser?
Send him to school.

What is Santa's favorite state to visit?
Ida Ho Ho Ho

Have you seen those traffic circles or
driven around them?
Well, they are pointless.

Why can't you hear a pterodactyl go to the bathroom?
The P is silent.

What's a dog's favorite super hero?
Labra-Thor.

I was walking down the beach when I heard a swimmer yelling for help with a shark circling him. I just laughed....I knew that shark wasn't going to help him.

What do you call a rabbit with fleas?
Bugs Bunny!

What do you say when a chicken is looking at salad?
Chicken sees a salad.

What do you call a cow with no legs?
Ground beef!

You are on a horse riding full gallop. Next to you is a giraffe at full gallop, and behind you is a lion on your tail. What do you do? Get off the carousel.

I had a horse named mayo, and mayo neighed.

What family does the zebra belong to? Can't say, none of the families in our neighborhood owns a zebra.

What is the cutest creature in the sea?
A cuddlefish.

What do you call an elephant
in a telephone booth?
Stuck.

A man walked into a bar with a parrot
on his shoulder. The bartender said, "Does
the animal talk?" And the parrot replied,
"I don't know."

What do you get when you cross a parrot with a caterpillar? A little walkie-talkie.

Why did the chicken cross the playground? To get to the other slide.

What do you call a deer with no eyes? No eye deer.

What do you call a fish with no eyes?
Fshhhh

A pony walks into a noisy bar and tries to order a beer. Bartender says "I can't hear you! You'll have to speak up!" Pony says: "Sorry! I'm a little horse!"

Why did the chicken cross the road?
To show the possum it could be done.

Why aren't dogs allowed in bars?
Because they can't control their licker!

Why don't fish play basketball?
Because they're scared of the net.

"Why do fathers take an extra pair of
socks when they go golfing?"
"In case they get a hole in one!"

"What does a sprinter eat before a race?"
"Nothing, they fast!"

"My dad told me a joke about boxing.
I guess I missed the punch line."

"I don't play soccer because I enjoy the
sport. I'm just doing it for kicks!"

Where do basketball players go when they need a uniform?
New Jersey.

Why don't football players were glasses?
It's a contact sport.

What's the best animal in soccer?
A score-pion.

What's the difference between
a quarterback and a baby?
One takes
a snap, one takes a nap.

I used to be addicted to basketball,
but I rebounded.

Why can't pigs play soccer?
They hog the ball.

Why shouldn't you play tennis in the jungle? Too many cheetahs.

What does a sports fan have in common with an angry chicken?
A foul mouth.

Why couldn't the baby score in basketball?
He was always dribbling.

"I'm afraid for the calendar.
Its days are numbered."

"My wife said I should do lunges to stay in shape. That would be a big step forward."

"Singing in the shower is fun until you get soap in your mouth. Then it's a soap opera."

"What do a tick and the Eiffel Tower have in common?"
"They're both Paris sites."

"What do you call a fish wearing a bowtie?"
"Sofishticated."

"How do you follow Will Smith in the snow?"
"You follow the fresh prints."

"If April showers bring May flowers,
what do May flowers bring?"
"Pilgrims."

"I thought the dryer was shrinking my
clothes. Turns out it was the refrigerator
all along."

"How does dry skin affect you at work?"
"You don't have any elbow grease to put
into it."

"What do you call a factory that makes okay products?"
"A satisfactory."

"Dear Math, grow up and solve your own problems."

"What did the janitor say when he jumped out of the closet?"
"Supplies!"

"Have you heard about the chocolate
record player?
It sounds pretty sweet."

"What did the ocean say to the beach?"
"Nothing, it just waved."

"Why do seagulls fly over the ocean?"
"Because if they flew over the bay, we'd
call them bagels."

"How does the moon cut his hair?"
"Eclipse it."

"What did one wall say to the other?"
"I'll meet you at the corner."

"What did the zero say to the eight?"
"That belt looks good on you."

"A skeleton walks into a bar and says,
'Hey, bartender.
I'll have one beer and a mop.'"

"Where do fruits go on vacation?"
"Pear-is!"

"I asked my dog what's two minus two.
He said nothing."

"What did Baby Corn say to Mama Corn?"
"Where's Pop Corn?"

"What's the best thing about Switzerland?"
"I don't know, but the flag is a big plus."

"Where do you learn to make a banana split?"
"Sundae school."

"What has more letters than
the alphabet?" "The post office!"

"Dad, did you get a haircut?"
"No, I got them all cut!"

"What do you call a poor Santa Claus?"
"St. Nickel-less."

"I got carded at a liquor store, and my Blockbuster card accidentally fell out. The cashier said never mind."

"Where do boats go when they're sick?"
"To the boat doc."

"I don't trust those trees. They seem kind of shady."

"My wife is really mad at the fact that I have no sense of direction. So I packed up my stuff and right!"

"How do you get a squirrel to like you? Act like a nut."

"Why don't eggs tell jokes? They'd crack each other up."

"I don't trust stairs. They're always up to something."

"What do you call someone with no body and no nose? Nobody knows."

"Did you hear the rumor about butter? Well, I'm not going to spread it!"

"Why couldn't the bicycle stand up by itself? It was two tired."

"What did one hat say to the other?"
"Stay here! I'm going on ahead."

"Why did Billy get fired from the banana factory? He kept throwing away the bent ones."

"Dad, can you put my shoes on?"
"No, I don't think they'll fit me."

"What does a lemon say when it answers the phone?"
"Yellow!"

"This graveyard looks overcrowded. People must be dying to get in."

"What kind of car does an egg drive?"
"A yolkswagen."

"Dad, can you put the cat out?"
"I didn't know it was on fire."

"How does a taco say grace?"
"Lettuce pray."

"What time did the man go to the dentist?
Tooth hurt-y."

"Why didn't the skeleton climb the
mountain?"
"It didn't have the guts."

"What do you call it when a snowman
throws a tantrum?"
"A meltdown."

"How many tickles does it take to make
an octopus laugh?
Ten tickles."

"I have a joke about chemistry,
but I don't think it will get a reaction."

"What does a bee use to brush its hair?"
"A honeycomb!"

"How do you make a tissue dance?
You put a little boogie in it."

"Why did the math book look so sad?
Because of all of its problems!"

"What kind of shoes do ninjas wear?
Sneakers!"

"How does a penguin build its house?
Igloos it together."

"How did Harry Potter get down the hill?"
"Walking. JK! Rowling."

"I used to be addicted to soap,
but I'm clean now."

"A guy walks into a bar... and he was disqualified from the limbo contest."

"You think swimming with sharks is expensive? Swimming with sharks cost me an arm and a leg."

"When two vegans get in an argument, is it still called a beef?"

"I ordered a chicken and an egg from Amazon.
I'll let you know..."

"Do you wanna box for your leftovers?"
"No, but I'll wrestle you for them."

"That car looks nice but the muffler seems exhausted."

"Shout out to my fingers. I can count on all of them."

"If a child refuses to nap, are they guilty of resisting a rest?"

"What country's capital is growing the fastest?"
"Ireland. Every day it's Dublin."

"I once had a dream I was floating in an ocean of orange soda. It was more of a fanta sea."

"A cheeseburger walks into a bar. The bartender says, 'Sorry, we don't serve food here.'"

"I once got fired from a canned juice company. Apparently I couldn't concentrate."

"I used to play piano by ear.
Now I use my hands."

"Have you ever tried to catch a fog?
I tried yesterday but I mist."

"I'm on a seafood diet.
I see food and I eat it."

"Why did the scarecrow win an award?
Because he was outstanding in his field."

"I made a pencil with two erasers.
It was pointless."

"How do you make a Kleenex dance?
Put a little boogie in it!"

"I'm reading a book about anti-gravity. It's impossible to put down!"

"Did you hear about the guy who invented the knock-knock joke? He won the 'no-bell' prize."

"I've got a great joke about construction, but I'm still working on it."

"I used to hate facial hair...but then it grew on me."

"I decided to sell my vacuum cleaner—it was just gathering dust!"

"I had a neck brace fitted years ago and I've never looked back since."

"You know, people say they pick their nose, but I feel like I was just born with mine."

"What's brown and sticky? A stick."

"Why can't you hear a psychiatrist using the bathroom? Because the 'P' is silent."

"What do you call an elephant that doesn't matter? An irrelephant."

"What do you get from a pampered cow? Spoiled milk."

"I like telling Dad jokes. Sometimes he laughs!"

"What's the best smelling insect?"
"A deodor-ant."

"I used to be a personal trainer.
Then I gave my too weak notice."

"Did I tell you the time I fell in love during
a backflip? I was heels over head!"

"If a child refuses to sleep during nap time, are they guilty of resisting a rest?"

"I ordered a chicken and an egg online. I'll let you know."

"If you see a crime at an Apple Store, does that make you an iWitness?"

"I'm so good at sleeping, I can do it with my eyes closed!"

"I was going to tell a time-traveling joke, but you guys didn't like it."

"What did the vet say to the cat?"
"How are you feline?"

"What do you call a lazy baby kangaroo?"
"A pouch potato!"

"What happens when M&M's can't agree on anything?"
"They reach an M-passe."

"What do you call a belt made of watches?"
"A waist of time."

"What happens when a strawberry gets run over crossing the street?"
"Traffic jam."

"What do you call a pony with a sore throat?"
"A little hoarse."

"Where do math teachers go on vacation?"
"Times Square."

"Whenever I try to eat healthy, a chocolate bar looks at me and Snickers."

"What does garlic do when it gets hot?"
"It takes its cloves off."

"What's a robot's favorite snack?"
"Computer chips."

"How much does it cost Santa to park his sleigh?"
"Nothing, it's on the house."

"Mountains aren't just funny. They're hill areas."

"What do clouds wear?"
"Thunderwear."

"Why are piggy banks so wise?"
"They're filled with common cents."

"Why is Peter Pan always flying?"
"He neverlands."

"How do you get a good price on a sled?"
"You have toboggan."

"How can you tell if a tree is a dogwood tree?"
"By its bark."

"I used to hate facial hair, but then it grew on me."

"It's inappropriate to make a 'dad joke' if you're not a dad. It's a faux pa."

"What do you call a hot dog on wheels?"
"Fast food!"

"Where do young trees go to learn?"
"Elementree school."

"Did you hear about the circus fire?
It was in tents."

"Can February March?
No, but April May!"

"How do lawyers say goodbye?
We'll be suing ya!"

"Wanna hear a joke about paper?
Never mind—it's tearable."

"What's the best way to watch a fly fishing tournament? Live stream."

"Spring is here! I got so excited I wet my plants."

"I could tell a joke about pizza, but it's a little cheesy."

"Don't trust atoms. They make up everything!"

"When does a joke become a dad joke? When it becomes apparent."

"I wouldn't buy anything with velcro. It's a total rip-off."

"What's an astronaut's favorite part
of a computer?
The space bar."

"Why are elevator jokes so classic
and good?
They work on many levels."

"Why do bees have sticky hair?
Because they use a honeycomb."

"Which state has the most streets?
Rhode Island."

"What did the coffee report to
the police? A mugging."

"What did the fish say when he
hit the wall?
Dam."

"Is this pool safe for diving?
It deep ends."

"If you see a crime happen at the Apple
store, what does it make you?"
"An iWitness."

Why are Saturday and Sunday
the strongest days?
They aren't weak-days.

There's a fine line between the numerator and denominator.

What instrument is found in the bathroom?
A tuba toothpaste.

Why don't trash collectors require any training?
They just pick it up as they go.

What did one eye say to the other?
Between you and me, something smells.

Did you hear about the restaurant
on the moon?
Decent food but no atmosphere.

What did the buffalo say as his son left?
Bison.

What do you call the horse that lives next door?
A neigh-bor.

I was wondering why the ball kept getting bigger and bigger, and then it hit me.

What did the leader of the hot dog race say to the others?
You better ketchup.

Why are elevator jokes so classic
and good?
They work on many levels.

How can you tell it's a dogwood tree?
By the bark.

What do you call it when a group of apes
starts a company?
Monkey business.

Why do bees have sticky hair?
They use a honeycomb.

Did you hear about the kidnapping
at school?
He eventually woke up.

My boss told me to have a good day,
so I went home.

If the early bird gets the worm,
then I think I'll just sleep in.

Why is Peter Pan always flying?
Because he Neverlands.

Two people walked into a bar.
The third ducked.

What car does a sheep drive?
A lamborghini.

Why are celebrities never sweating?
They're surrounded by fans.

Which state gives you the smallest beverages?
Minnesota.

Why don't fruits have weddings?
Because they cantaloupe.

Why are goldfish the most dangerous animal?
Because they live in a tank.

What's the only shape to ever be knighted?
Circles.

Sore throats are a pain in the neck.

What does a house wear?
Address.

I like telling Dad jokes... sometimes he laughs.

Printed in Great Britain
by Amazon

51861688R00057